23.00po

P9-ELW-714

T 283331

A Taste
of culture

Foods of Kenya

Barbara Sheen

KIDHAVEN PRESS
An imprint of Thomson Gale, a part of The Thomson Corporation

GALE
CENGAGE Learning

Detroit • New York • San Francisco • New Haven, Conn • Waterville, Maine • London

© 2010 Gale, Cengage Learning

LIBRARY OF CONGRESS CATALOGING-IN-PUBLICATION DATA

Sheen, Barbara.
  Foods of Kenya / by Barbara Sheen.
    p. cm. -- (A taste of culture)
  Includes bibliographical references and index.
  ISBN 978-0-7377-4813-0 (hardcover)
  1. Cookery, Kenyan--Juvenile literature. 2. Kenya--Social life and customs--Juvenile literature. I. Title.
  TX725.K39S54 2010
  641.596762--dc22

                                                      2009048378

Kidhaven Press
27500 Drake Rd.
Farmington Hills MI 48331

ISBN-13: 978-0-7377-4813-0
ISBN-10: 0-7377-4813-3

Printed in the United States of America
1 2 3 4 5 6 7 14 13 12 11 10

Printed by Bang Printing, Brainerd, MN, 1st Ptg., 04/2010

Contents

Chapter 1

A Land of Contrasts

Kenya is a land of contrasts. Grassy savannahs teeming with wild animals, sparkling blue lakes, an extinct volcano, tropical beaches, a lush rain forest, fertile valleys, and dry arid lands that barely support life all are a part of Kenya.

Kenya's population, too, is diverse. The people of Kenya have different cultural backgrounds, practice many different religions, speak a number of different languages, and live in different ways. Many reside in the nation's bustling modern cities, while others follow a traditional tribal lifestyle. In fact, it takes only a few hours to travel from Nairobi, Kenya's capital city, to a rural village where spear-carrying Masai (Mah-sigh)

AFRICA

FOOD REGIONS OF KENYA

SUDAN

ETHIOPIA

UGANDA

KENYA

Kitale

Nairobi

Mombasa

TANZANIA

INDIAN OCEAN

Fish

Vegetables

Rice

Potatoes

Beans

Tea

Coffee

Cattle

Corn

warriors raise cattle in much the same way their ancestors did.

Despite these contrasts, Kenyans have much in common, especially when it comes to the food they

The Masai of Kenya still follow a traditional tribal lifestyle, similar to that of their ancestors.

eat. Kenyan cooks depend on three basic ingredients—corn, leafy greens, and fruit. These important staples tie all Kenyans together.

A Popular Crop

Starches, like corn, rice, and potatoes, play a key role in Kenyan cooking, with corn being far and away the most popular. Corn, which is also known in Kenya as **maize**, first arrived in East Africa in the 16th century when Portuguese slave traders brought it here from the Americas.

Corn grows well in Kenya's warm climate. Soon Kenyans came to depend upon it. Food historian Reay

About Kenya

Kenya is located in East Africa. It is the 47th largest country in the world. Its official languages are English and Swahili. It is bordered by Ethiopia and Somalia to the north, Tanzania to the south, Uganda and Sudan to the west, and the Indian Ocean to the southeast. Kenya's highest peak, Mount Kenya, is an extinct volcano. It is also the second highest mountain peak in Africa.

Mount Kenya is located in the Rift Valley. It formed along a 3,106-mile-long (4,999km) fault in the earth's crust. The area contains extinct volcanoes, lakes, hot springs, and geysers.

Kenya's largest city, Nairobi, is located south of the Rift Valley. It is the home of more than 2 million people. It is the financial and communication hub of East Africa.

Corn, or maize, grows well in Kenya's warm climate and is used in several dishes.

Tannahill explains, "A woman working alone could plant her [corn] seeds, leave them to grow and harvest the crop as and when she needed it; when one patch of soil became exhausted, she moved on to another. It was poor agriculture, but it sustained life and made few demands."[1]

Cornfields are a common sight in modern Kenya. Corn is grown in almost every **shamba** (shahm-bah), or garden. According to Iris Hunt of the Mount Kenya Wildlife Conservatory in Nanyuki, Kenya, "driving along country roads, you will see corn growing everywhere. . . . Any Kenyan's dream is to have a small 'shamba' and the first thing he will plant is corn for the family."[2]

Many Uses

Kenyans use corn in many different ways. They roast it, boil it, grill it, and fry it. They grind it into corn flour. And they dry it to make **samp**, or hominy. Drying the corn preserves it, so that it can be kept for long periods without spoiling.

Uji (you-jee) is a thin porridge made with cornmeal. Kenyans of all ages like to have a steaming bowl of it topped with milk for breakfast. It has a sweet, pleasant taste similar to Cream of Wheat. Uji is the first solid food most Kenyan babies eat.

Corn is also used to make crispy fritters and chewy dumplings. It is a key ingredient in the many stews that Kenyans love. Most importantly, corn is used to make **ugali** (you-gah-lee), a cornmeal mush that is served at every meal.

Ugali, which is known as fufu in other parts of Africa, is a mixture of cornmeal and water. It is cooked until it becomes a thick, spongy block similar in texture to grits. Because ugali hardens as it cools, it is always

A mother and her children grind corn.

Ugali

Making ugali requires a lot of stirring so the ugali does not stick to the pot. Milk may be substituted for the water or a mixture of milk and water may be used. Ugali should be eaten hot. It hardens as it cools.

Ingredients
1 cup cornmeal
2 cups water

Directions
1. Put the water in a saucepan and bring to a boil.
2. Stir in the cornmeal. Lower heat to medium-low. Cook until the mixture is thick, stirring constantly, about 15 minutes.
3. Cover the pot and simmer for another 5 minutes. The ugali is done when it pulls away from the side of the pot and sticks together.
4. Place the ugali in a large bowl. Either break off pieces by hand or scoop out little balls with an ice cream scoop.

Serves 3 to 4.

served hot. Kenyans, who traditionally do not use utensils, use their fingers to break off chunks of ugali, which they roll into golf-ball-size spheres. Then they make a hole in the center of the ugali with their thumb and use it to scoop up bits of stew or meat.

Ugali is quite filling. It has a bland taste that takes on the flavors of whatever foods it is eaten with. Kenyans cannot do without it. According to journalist John Makeni, "a meal without it is considered . . . no meal at all."[3]

Leafy Greens

Leafy greens, such as spinach, cabbage, kale, collard greens, and potato and pumpkin leaves, make up another important part of the Kenyan diet. They go well with ugali and add color, flavor, and essential nutrients to stews and soups.

Kenyans cook greens with beans, corn, squash, tomatoes, potatoes, and other vegetables. They mix them with fried onions, boil them in coconut milk, and top them with peanuts. They stew them with chunks of beef and eat them without other accompaniments.

Kenyan Wildlife

Kenya is the home of many animals. To protect these animals from hunters, Kenya has 35 wildlife reserves. People from all over the world visit Kenya to see African wildlife in their natural habitat in these reserves.

Elephants, rhinoceroses, lions, giraffes, leopards, cheetahs, hyenas, wild dogs, monkeys, and huge herds of zebras, gazelles, and wildebeests all live in these reserves.

Kenyan wildebeests are famous for their mass migrations. Millions travel across Kenya every summer and fall in search of fresh grass.

Crocodiles, snakes, baboons, hippos, flamingos, herons, great white egrets, and other exotic animals are also found in Kenya. In fact, one-third of the world's flamingo population nests in Kenya. It is possible to see more than 2 million flamingos at one time around Kenya's Lake Nakuru.

Kale is another popular vegetable that is used to add color, flavor, and nutrients to stews and soups.

Greens grow in much of the countryside. Gathering them is a common practice. Greens also have a place in almost every Kenyan's garden and have been cultivated here for hundreds of years. Kenyans prize greens for their flavor and because they are economical.

In fact, **sukuma wiki** (sue-kue-mah wee-kee), a favorite Kenyan dish which features kale, literally means "stretch the week." Kale is easily available and inexpensive. Using it as the main ingredient in stew when money is tight and other foods are unavailable can keep a family fed until payday.

Besides kale, sukuma wiki also contains tomatoes

and onions. Other ingredients may be added to the stew depending on what is available. That is the beauty of cooking with greens. They go well with almost everything, so cooks can improvise with whatever ingredients they have on hand and still create a delicious meal.

Tropical Fruit

Fruits of all kinds are another mainstay of the Kenyan diet. Trees loaded with fragrant and juicy tropical fruits

Sukuma Wiki

Sukuma wiki is usually made with kale. Spinach or collard greens can be substituted for kale. Chicken or beef and other vegetables, such as squash, may also be added. Sukuma wiki is tasty served over rice.

Ingredients
½ pound kale, cleaned and chopped
1 small onion, peeled and chopped
2 tablespoons tomato paste
2 tablespoons olive oil
½ bell pepper, chopped
salt and pepper to taste
garlic powder to taste

Directions
1. Heat the oil in a large frying pan over medium heat, add the onion and cook until it is soft.
2. Add the tomato paste, bell pepper, garlic, and salt and pepper. If adding beef or chicken, add it now as well. Cook for about 5 minutes.
3. Add the kale. Cover the pan. Cook on low for 5 minutes.
Serves 4.

grow wild throughout much of the Kenyan countryside except in the arid northeast. Most gardens have at least one fruit tree and many have more. Large farms cultivate pineapple, which is one of Kenya's major cash crops.

Every Kenyan city and town has a market made up of wood stalls piled high with a wide array of brightly colored, incredibly fragrant fresh fruits, many of which are

Every Kenyan city has a market made up of wood stalls that are piled high with fruits.

brought into town by women who carry bulging sacks of fruit on their backs. "We are lucky here in Kenya," Hunt explains. "Fruit is abundant all year round. . . . There are fruit stands everywhere offering freshly picked produce from the immediate neighborhood that day."[4]

Most Kenyans eat fresh fruit two or three times a day. Eating fruit is the customary way to end a meal. Fruit is also made into juices and smoothies, used in salads, and served with ice cream. Some of these fruits are recognizable to Americans, while others are less familiar. There are sweet, orange-fleshed papayas; tart, jellylike passion fruits; creamy avocados; citrus fruits of all kinds; juicy mangoes; cream-color, semisweet baobabs, whose seeds are coated with sugar and eaten like candy; and delicious bananas.

The variety of bananas alone is astounding. Dwarf bananas that taste like apples, finger-size red bananas, long yellow bananas, small green **matokes** (mah-toh-kees), and starchy **plantains** (plan-tains) are only some of the many types.

Plantains, in particular, are a local favorite. They are larger than other bananas and must be cooked before

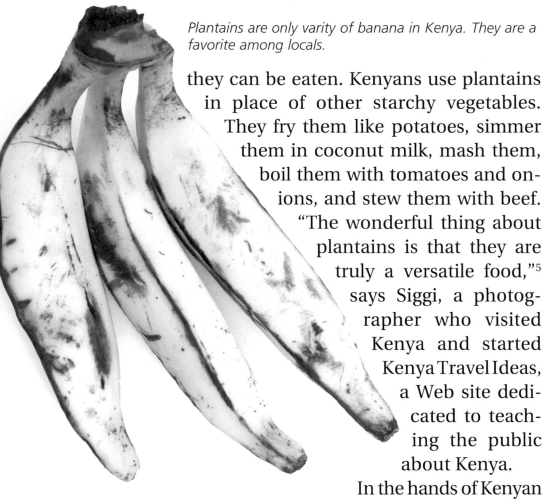

Plantains are only varity of banana in Kenya. They are a favorite among locals.

they can be eaten. Kenyans use plantains in place of other starchy vegetables. They fry them like potatoes, simmer them in coconut milk, mash them, boil them with tomatoes and onions, and stew them with beef. "The wonderful thing about plantains is that they are truly a versatile food,"[5] says Siggi, a photographer who visited Kenya and started Kenya Travel Ideas, a Web site dedicated to teaching the public about Kenya.

In the hands of Kenyan cooks fruits, greens, and corn are all versatile foods. These staples are the flavor of Kenya. They help bind this diverse nation together.

Many Influences

Many different groups have played a role in Kenya's history. Tribal groups from South, West, and North Africa began arriving and settling in Kenya around 1000 A.D. The spice trade brought Arab traders here in the 8th century. They built towns along the Indian Ocean and intermarried with native Kenyans, creating a cultural group known as the **Swahili** (Swaheel-ee).

European traders, too, visited the coast. In the16th century the Portuguese took control of many coastal towns. About 150 years later, the British arrived and claimed Kenya as a British colony. British settlers built farms in the highlands near Nairobi. They brought indentured servants from India with them who worked

Kenyan Tribal Groups

About 40 different tribal groups live in Kenya. Those that came from West Africa speak Bantu. They include the Kikuyu, Meru, Gusii, Embu, Akamba, Luyha, Kamba, Mijikenda, among others. In the past, the members of these tribes were farmers. Today most of these tribes have adopted a Western lifestyle. They work in businesses, banks, schools, and hospitals, to name a few of the ways they earn a living. Members of the Kikuyu, the largest tribe in Kenya, dominate Kenyan politics.

A number of other tribes came from North Africa. They share the Nilotic language. These tribes include the Masai, Samburu, Luo, and Turkana. In the past these people were nomadic herdsmen who raised goats, sheep, camels, and cattle. Most of the Masai, Samburu, and Turkana people still maintain this traditional lifestyle, while the Luo lead a modern lifestyle. Other groups that migrated from Somalia and Ethiopia have also kept their traditional lifestyle. These groups include the Rendille, Oram, and Somali, all of whom speak Cushitic.

on their farms and were instrumental in building the railroad that connects Kenya and Uganda.

Kenya became an independent nation in 1963. But the influence of all these cultural groups remains strong. According to an article on Magical Kenya, Kenya's official tourism Web site, "Kenya has drawn on all these influences to develop its own unique culture. This is the nation's greatest strength—the ability to blend the best of many worlds into a strong singular identity."[6]

Kenya's favorite dishes reflect the influence of the

many cultural groups that are a part of Kenya, but they also have a unique Kenyan touch.

Creative Stews and Mashes

Kenyan cooks rarely follow recipes. They add, subtract, and change ingredients depending on what they have on hand. In this way, they have taken dishes brought to Kenya by different cultural groups and made them their own. Among the most popular of these dishes are a variety of stews and mashed vegetable dishes that developed in West Africa and were brought to Kenya by

Irio is a favorite dish among Kenyans, made of potatoes, corn, and beans.

Irio

Irio can be made with almost any type of bean, black-eyed peas, or green peas. This recipe uses kidney beans.

Ingredients
⅔ cup canned kidney beans
⅔ cup frozen or fresh corn kernels
4 small potatoes, washed, peeled, and cut into chunks
⅔ cup chopped spinach
2 tablespoons butter or margarine
salt and pepper to taste
water to cover

Directions
1. Place the kidney beans, corn, potatoes, and spinach in a large pot with enough water to cover the contents.
2. Cook over low heat until the potatoes are soft.
3. Drain the water out of the pot. Transfer the contents to a large bowl and add the butter, salt, and pepper. Mash the ingredients together.
4. Serve with lemon wedges.
Serves 4 to 6.

Kenya's largest ethnic group, the Kikuyu (Kee-coo-you) tribe.

Irio (ee-ree-o), which is the Kikuyu word for food, is a favorite among all Kenyans. It is a hearty dish made of potatoes mashed with corn and beans. The Kikuyu people traditionally combine corn and beans in their cooking. Doing so is very nutritious. It provides the same quality of protein as meat or fish.

There are almost as many ways to prepare irio as there are Kenyan cooks. Irio almost always starts with potatoes, corn, and beans, but then Kenyan cooks add any number of other ingredients to the dish. Spinach, fried onions, vegetables, and chunks of meat are all popular additions. Coastal cooks often add seafood. "This dish . . . is wonderfully versatile," explains author Dorinda Hafner. "An innovative cook can make much of irio, adding different flavorings such as garlic, fresh herbs, and spices, combining it with dried salted fish, seafood, or minced meat, or stuffing it into various vegetables."[7] Indeed, versatility is what makes traditional dishes such as irio distinctly Kenyan.

Irio is both a main dish and a popular accompaniment to grilled meat. **Githeri** (ghee-thay-ree) is also eaten as both a meal and as a side dish. It is another popular stew with Kikuyu roots. Githeri is a combination of boiled corn and beans. In rural villages, it is often cooked in large pots over a wood fire, which adds an

Githeri, another popular stew, is served in a hollowed out goard called a calabash.

earthy flavor to the stew. Traditionally it is served in a calabash, a large gourd that is hollowed out and used as a bowl.

As with all Kenyan stews, the ingredients are flexible. Some cooks substitute samp, or dried corn, for fresh corn in githeri. This changes the texture of the stew, making it smoother and creamier. Some cooks add chunks of meat and onions.

Kenyan cooks are equally creative when they make groundnut stew, another local favorite. The idea of cooking with groundnuts, which is what Kenyans call peanuts, has West African roots. Kenya's Kikuyu, Luhya (Looh-ah), and Meru (May-roo) tribes, all of which

A Useful Nut

Coconuts are believed to have originated on islands in the South Pacific. Historians theorize that Malaysian seamen brought the nut to Madagascar, an East African island in the first century A.D. From here, the nut probably floated to East Africa.

Today there are about 7.4 million coconut trees in Kenya. Some are cultivated on coconut farms, while many grow wild along Kenya's coast. Besides using coconut meat in their cooking, the Swahili people carve the shells into bowls, serving spoons, earrings, and hair clips. Fiber from the shell is used to make rope.

The Swahili also weave the leaves of coconut trees together to make thatched roofs for their houses. This type of roof keeps houses cool in the coastal heat and can be replaced when needed.

came to Kenya from West Africa, claim groundnut stew in one form or another as their own.

Unsalted peanuts and onions stewed in water are the foundations of the dish. Then the fun begins. Spinach or pumpkin leaves may be added to the bubbling pot. Sometimes the stew is cooked in coconut milk, which gives it a rich sweet taste. Chili peppers may also be tossed in. Cooking with coconut milk and chili peppers is a Swahili custom that many Kenyan cooks have embraced. In a nod to Kenya's Indian population, other hot spices may be added too.

Curries and Chapati

Indian immigrants brought curry to Kenya. Curry is not a single dish but a variety of stewlike dishes bathed in a spicy sauce. These dishes have different main ingredients, but the basis of every one is a zesty sauce made from a blend of aromatic spices. Which spices are used and in what quantity depends on the chef. Because curry recipes are so adaptable, they are perfect for freewheeling Kenyan cooks. They have added their own touches to this Indian favorite and made it a Kenyan favorite too.

To make curry, cooks grind any number of spices, such as cumin, mustard seeds, fennel seeds, peppercorns, and cayenne pepper, into a powder. Such spices first arrived in Kenya with early Arab traders. The Swahili people have always used spices in their cooking, and Kenyan curries have a distinct Swahili influence. Kenyan curry is usually cooked in coconut milk, which

Curry was brought to Kenya by Indian immigrants, and is a zesty spice commonly used among Kenyan cooks.

makes it smoother, sweeter, and creamier than most Indian curries. And Kenyan cooks like to add slices of mango and other tropical fruits to their curry—another Swahili touch.

Main ingredients vary wildly. Everything from crocodile meat to eggplant is used. On the coast, fish rules. Vegetable curries and lamb curries are also quite popular. Pranay B. Gupte, an Indian journalist, says that the lamb curry he ate in Kenya was "the best lamb curry I have had anywhere."[8]

Curry dishes are almost always served with **chapati** (cha-pah-tee), soft flatbread perfect for sopping up stews and sauces. It is the most popular bread in Kenya. The bread has it roots in India, but Kenyan cooks have changed it by rolling and coiling the dough repeatedly before baking the bread, which produces a flaky layered bread unique to Kenya.

Grilled Meat

Nyama choma (ah-mah cho-mah), or grilled meat, is another favorite Kenyan dish. In fact, it may be the Kenyan people's favorite main dish. Grilling is one of the oldest ways to cook meat. Almost every tribal group in Kenya has a long history of cooking meat over an open fire. Early Arab settlers, too, brought their tradition of barbecuing to Kenya.

The meat used for nyama choma is incredibly fresh. Traveling markets in which cattle are bought, sold, and butchered and where nyama choma is served are found all over Kenya. Slabs of fresh meat are hung from poles.

Nyama choma, a popular meat dish among Kenyans.

Customers inspect the meat and choose the piece they want. It is cut, weighed, and then grilled over a charcoal fire. Even many upscale restaurants have butcheries on-site. "You select your meat, then it is tossed on the barbie [barbecue]—any day of the week you'll see clouds of delicious smelling smoke rising from the restaurant,"[9] notes one restaurant review on the Lonely Planet Web site.

Before it is grilled, the meat is sprinkled with spices.

When the meat is done, it is cut into small chunks and placed in a bowl. It is served with another bowl filled with salt. Diners dip the meat into the salt and enjoy the smoky meaty flavor. Chapati and irio are often served on the side.

Although beef is the most popular meat used in nyama choma, Kenyan cooks are creative in what they

Groundnut Stew

This recipe adds spinach to groundnut stew. Chicken or meat and other vegetables may be added.

Ingredients
⅔ cup unsalted peanuts, shelled and chopped fine
10 ounces frozen chopped spinach, thawed
1 small onion, chopped
1 cup coconut milk
1 jalapeño pepper, chopped
1 tablespoon peanut or olive oil
1 pinch garlic
salt and pepper to taste

Directions
1. Put the oil in a frying pan. Add the onions and jalapeño pepper and cook over medium heat, until the onions are golden.
2. Stir in the peanuts and coconut milk. Keep stirring until the mixture boils.
3. Reduce the heat to low. Add the spinach, garlic, and salt and pepper. Cover the pan and cook until the spinach is cooked.
Serves 4.

Masai grilling beef over an open fire at a cattle market.

use. Goat, lamb, zebra, and antelope are also prepared in this way. Indeed, whether it be grilled meat, stews and mashes, or curries and bread, Kenyan cooks are known for their creativity. They have taken foods and cooking styles brought to Kenya by people of many cultures and turned them into uniquely Kenyan dishes. It is no wonder that Kenyans love these dishes.

All Kinds of Snacks

Kenyans like to snack. Street vendors, roadside stands, juice bars, and cafés all serve up tempting snacks in both liquid and solid form. Popular favorites include fresh-squeezed juice, spiced tea, **maandazi** (mah-an-dah-zee), and **sambusa** (sam-boo-sah).

Delicious Juices

Kenya straddles the equator. In the lowlands, summer temperatures can reach 98°F (37°C). A glass of icy cold fruit juice is a perfect thirst quencher on a blistering Kenyan afternoon. Juice bars, which may be modern shops in large shopping malls, wooden market stalls, or street carts, are popular gathering places for thirsty Kenyans. They visit them day and night to get a healthy

Sweet Snacks

When Kenyans crave a sweet snack, they have lots of interesting choices, such as ice cream and yogurt. They are sold in little stores and stands.

Sweet roasted corn on the cob is also popular. Street vendors roast corn on wire grills over a charcoal fire. It is a common sight to see Kenyan children eating corn, especially in small towns and rural areas.

Deep-fried yams are another sweet treat popular with young Kenyans. The hot potatoes are drizzled with lime juice and sprinkled with chili powder.

Sugar cane is another favorite. Vendors use a sharp knife to cut back the outer stalk of the cane so that customers can get to the inner stalk, which contains sugary juice. Snackers chew on the inner stalk like gum. As they chew, the juice is released. They do not swallow the chewed stalk since it is too fiberous to eat.

liquid snack. Authors Joseph Bindloss, Tom Parkinson, and Matt Fletcher explain, "With all the fresh fruit on offer in Kenya, fruit juices are a national obsession and the best on offer are breathtakingly good."[10]

The number of choices is almost endless. Tangerine, mango, pineapple, melon, papaya, sugar cane, and passion fruit juice are all very popular, with passion fruit juice being a national favorite. Known to Kenyans simply as "passion," the juice has a refreshingly tart flavor that Kenyans cannot get enough of. It also has a sweet enticing aroma and is loaded with vitamins A and C and iron. In addition, passion fruit contains natural chemicals that have a calming effect on the body. Kenyans say drinking it relaxes them.

Creative Kenyans often combine passion fruit and other juices to make tantalizingly different mixed juices. Any combination of fruits can become juice in Kenya. The mixtures are limited only by the cook's imagination.

To make juice, fresh fruit is mixed in a blender with crushed ice and water. Sometimes sugar is added. Smoothies, in which milk or yogurt is substituted for water, are also popular. But juice reigns supreme. Robin Kear, a librarian who worked for a short time in Nairobi, says, "My friends love, love, love fresh juice . . . not that I am complaining. Fresh juice is delicious."[11]

Passion fruit juice is a national favorite loaded with vitamins A and C. It is also very aromatic.

Many Challenges

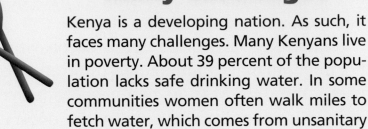

Kenya is a developing nation. As such, it faces many challenges. Many Kenyans live in poverty. About 39 percent of the population lacks safe drinking water. In some communities women often walk miles to fetch water, which comes from unsanitary wells. Poverty also keeps some children from attending school. Their parents cannot afford to pay for the required uniforms or books.

Disease is also a problem. Human immunodeficiency virus (HIV) and acquired immunodeficiency syndrome (AIDS) are common here. Although the percentage of Kenyans suffering from HIV and AIDS has dropped recently, there are currently about 900,000 orphans in Kenya, many of whom lost their parents to AIDS. A shortage of medical doctors worsens the problem.

Sweet Milky Tea

A soothing cup of sweet milky tea, or chai (cha-ee) as it is known here, is another popular liquid snack. Tea is important to Kenya's economy. It is grown in the highlands near Mount Kenya, an extinct volcano. Kenya is the world's third-largest producer and the top exporter of black tea.

Kenyan tea is famous throughout the world. It has a brisk flavor, dark color, and an enchanting aroma, which experts say is due to the volcanic soil in which it is grown. Women wearing large sacks slung across their backs harvest the tea by hand. They make sure to pick only the choicest upper leaves. This ensures that the

Kenyans drink tea throughout the day. Kenyan tea is famous for its aroma, dark color, and brisk flavor.

tea does not taste bitter.

Kenyans drink tea day and night. Many Kenyans take a morning tea break. Afternoon teatime, a custom Kenyans have retained from British colonial times, is also popular. In fact, if you visit a Kenyan home, you will probably find a teakettle on the stove. It is considered rude not to share tea with visitors, and guests are always offered at least one cup. And when friends and

Spiced Chai

Spiced chai is simple to make. More or less spices or sugar may be used. Kenyans use about double the sugar this recipe calls for. Kenyan milk is thick and rich. Full-fat milk is closest to the milk Kenyans use.

Ingredients
½ cup water
1 cup whole milk
2 teaspoons black tea or 2 tea bags
4 teaspoons sugar
½ teaspoon cinnamon
½ teaspoon ginger or cardamom

Directions
1. Bring the water to boil in a saucepan.
2. Add the milk, tea, sugar, and spices, and stir well. Bring the mixture to a boil over medium heat.
3. Turn off the heat, cover the pot, and let the tea steep. The longer it steeps, the stronger and darker the tea gets.
4. Strain the mixture. Pour into a teapot or individual cups and serve.
Serves 2.

relatives drop in, they often bring tea along as a hostess gift. Rachel Ngondo, a Kenyan business executive explains, "In a typical Kenyan home, you will be offered tea any time you visit. . . . In rural areas, there will always be a pot of tea in the fire because any time is tea time. . . . Tea symbolizes hospitality in Kenya."[12]

What is inside the teakettle is interesting. First, water is brought to a boil. Then milk, tea, and lots of sugar are added to the pot. Four or five teaspoons of sugar per cup of tea is not unusual. "Chai must be made sweet so that the lips stick together,"[13] claims one recipe for chai posted on the African Wanderings Web site.

Once the milk, tea, and sugar are added, the mixture is boiled again. This causes the milk to get foamy. Many Kenyans like to add spices, such as cinnamon, cardamom, ginger, and cloves, to the teakettle much like people in India do. This gives the tea a fragrance similar to that of hot pumpkin pie.

Whether spiced or plain, Kenyans cannot get enough chai. It is sold in cafés, restaurants, and little chai stalls. It is served at business meetings, at social gatherings, in schools, and in homes. According to writer Jeanne Egbosiuba Ukwendu, "it is the beverage choice of Kenya."[14]

Fried Pastry

Tea is often accompanied by pastry called maandazi (mahn-dah-zee). It is made of fried dough and looks like a small, flat doughnut. But maandazi is not as sweet as a doughnut. It does not have to be, since it is

Maandazi

Maandazi tastes best when it is eaten warm. As it cools, it hardens. It can be made with white or wheat flour. Coconut milk may be substituted for milk.

Ingredients
2 cups flour
2 teaspoons baking powder
1 egg, beaten
½ cup milk
2 tablespoons melted butter or margarine
⅔ cup sugar
1 teaspoon cinnamon
1 pinch salt
oil for frying

Directions
1. Mix the flour, baking powder, sugar, cinnamon, and salt in a bowl.
2. Mix the egg, milk, and butter together in another bowl. Add it to the flour mixture and mix well until a smooth, soft, dough forms. If the dough is sticky, add more flour.
3. Cover the dough with a clean towel and let it sit in a warm place for 30 minutes.
4. Flour a cutting board. Roll the dough out on the board until it is about 1/2-inch thick.
5. Cut the dough into squares or triangles.
6. Heat the oil in a frying pan over medium heat. When the oil is hot, fry the maandazi. When it is golden on one side, turn it over.
7. When the maandazi is golden on both sides, remove it from the pan and place it between clean paper towels to drain. Continue frying the maandazi until all the dough is used.

Makes about 24 pastries. Serves 12.

usually served with supersweet chai. Maandazi has a semisweet taste and a chewy texture.

The fried treat has a delightful scent that comes from the cardamom that flavors the dough. Some cooks add shredded coconut to the dough or substitute coconut milk for traditional milk. This adds to the pastry's perfume and gives it an exotic taste. Some cooks dust the pastry with sugar.

Maandazi is always served warm. It is eaten for breakfast and as a snack. According to Ukwendu, "you can find these delicious doughnuts in large urban areas and also among the Swahili people. . . . Most small restaurants . . . serve mandazi [maandazi]. You can also find mandazi being sold by street vendors."[15]

Sambusas

Sambusas (sam-boo-sahs) are another fried treat that street vendors tempt hungry passersby with. Sambusa vendors can be found on almost every street corner in Kenya's cities and towns. Kenyans throng their stands in an effort to get their fill of this savory delicacy.

But sambusas are not just street food. They are served in cafés, fine restaurants, and homes across Kenya, as well as at weddings, charity events, and fancy government receptions. African cookbook author Harva Hachten recalls that the first time she tasted sambusas was at "a reception in Kenya hosted by the minister of information in the beautiful gardens of the Parliament Building."[16]

Sambusas came to Kenya via India, where they are

Sambusas, a popular fried sweet treat, are made of flaky dough and filled with anything from ground beef to fruit.

Sambusas can not only be purchased from vendors on street corners, but also in resort restaurants.

known as Samosas. They are small, triangular pastries that are stuffed with anything and everything. Ground beef and onions, potatoes and vegetables, and fruits all find their way into Kenyan sambusas. All are seasoned with an aromatic and delicious blend of spices. The flavor combinations depend on the cook's imagination. Combinations like chili, mint, cinnamon, cardamom, and cloves are popular. Kenyan cooks are careful to balance the spices, using just enough of each so that no taste or fragrance overwhelms another.

Making good sambusas takes care. The dough must be thin and flaky. To get it right, it must be rolled out repeatedly. Once the dough is paper-thin, it is cut into small circles, which are heated on a griddle. Next, each circle is folded like a little cone and filled with stuffing, which has been prepared separately. The top of each cone is folded over and sealed with water, forming a cute little triangular pouch that is fried in hot oil until it is crisp and golden.

The results are well worth the effort. It is hard to eat just one. So most Kenyans eat several. Indeed, with delicious foods like spicy sambusas, warm maandazi, sweet milky chai and freshly squeezed juices sold everywhere, it is no wonder Kenyans love to snack. These tempting delights are hard to resist.

Welcome! Welcome!

Hospitality and generosity are a way of life in Kenya. No visit is complete without mountains of food. Holidays and special occasions bring crowds of friends and relatives to festive meals. But even regular meals and tea breaks become special occasions when guests arrive. An article on the Web site KIDSICO, a Kenyan organization working to improve education, health care, and the economy of West Kenya, explains that "Kenyans are generous people. They will always offer food and soda to guests. If you visit more than one home in a day, be prepared to eat a full meal at each. . . . Kenyans take pride in being able to provide food for visitors and will always encourage you to eat, eat, eat!"[17]

Kenyans welcome travelers with great hospitality and generosity. Many Europeans travel to the country for the holidays.

Christmas Chicken

Kenyans celebrate many holidays. More than half the population is Christian. For them, Christmas is a time to get together and celebrate. Many city dwellers flock to rural areas to spend the holiday with their relatives. Their arrival is greeted with lots of food.

Christmas dinner menus vary. But it is likely that chicken in some form will find its way to the holiday table. Chickens are not as commonplace in Kenya as in most industrialized nations. While cattle are raised throughout Kenya, there are few commercial chicken farms. Many rural people keep a few chickens in their yards, but these animals are treasured for the eggs they produce. They are rarely slaughtered unless it is a special occasion.

Chicken is not a common food in Kenya, but is almost always served at Christmas. Kenyans most often buy their chickens live, as seen here by this vendor.

If a Kenyan purchases a chicken at a butcher shop, the animal is almost always purchased live. Most cooks slaughter and pluck the bird themselves.

Kenyan chickens are free-range. This means they roam outdoors rather than being kept in small cages. They eat natural foods that are not treated with hormones, antibiotics, or other chemicals. Many people say this makes the chickens tastier and nutritionally healthier.

Sharing Festive Dishes

Kenyans use chicken in a variety of festive dishes. **Kuku na nazi** (kou-kou nah nah-zee), or chicken in coconut milk, is a popular favorite created by the

How Kenyans Live

Most Kenyans have a modern lifestyle. They wear Western-style clothes and use high-tech devices, like cell phones and computers.

In the cities many Kenyans live in high-rise apartment buildings. Private homes are usually made of concrete blocks and have roofs made of tile or iron sheets. Many rural homes are made of mud. Although some Kenyans have modern kitchens with a gas or electric stove, many rural Kenyans cook on little stoves heated with charcoal.

Large cities have big supermarkets and shopping malls. Small towns have little stores that sell groceries and other items. Cities and towns have outdoor markets where fresh produce, spices, fish, and meat are sold.

Many Kenyans own cars. Small buses also provide transportation. A train runs from Kenya to Uganda.

Soccer is the most popular sport in Kenya. Rap, reggae, and rock music are popular.

Swahili people. It combines chicken and onions with fragrant spices, coconut milk, and coconut cream. Coconut cream is the thick layer that forms on top of chilled coconut milk. The mixture is cooked slowly, so that the different flavors can blend together in perfect harmony. The result is a rich, creamy, and exotic dish that smells of the tropics and tastes delicious.

Karamu (kah-rah-moo) chicken is another celebratory chicken dish. For this dish, chicken is cooked with French salad dressing and then bathed in a zesty sauce made from even more French salad dressing, tomatoes, onions, celery, black pepper, and sweet paprika. Karamu is the Swahili word for "feast." Whenever karamu chicken is served in Kenya, a celebration is sure to follow. Because of its place on festive tables in Kenya and because of the meaning of its name, many African Americans serve it for Kwanzaa.

Chicken is also grilled like beef to make kuku choma. It is fried in hot oil, made into curry, and turned into countless stews. Chicken is usually boiled whole in

Coconut milk is used in several Kenyan dishes and provides a sweet taste.

stews, then cut into little pieces small enough to be eaten with the fingers. For festive meals, it is usually served on a central tray, which everyone eats from. No individual plates are used. Kenyans say this type of sharing brings everyone closer together and makes them feel more welcome. "Everyone, young and old, reaches into the sinia [central tray] with their hands, laughing and telling stories. . . . My favorite aspect . . . is that it is a communal affair,"[18] says Kenyan chef James Mbugna.

The Masai

The Masai may be the most famous tribal group in Africa. Many people have seen pictures of tall, spear-carrying Masai men wearing a red cloth wrapped around their waist or shoulders.

The Masai live a traditional lifestyle centered on herding cattle. Members of the tribe measure their wealth by the number of cattle they own. They rarely kill cattle for food. They get meat protein by drinking small amounts of blood, which they drain from the animals, mixed with milk. This does not hurt the cattle.

The Masai live in small settlements surrounded by thorn-bush fences. The fences keep the cattle safe from predators at night. The tribe's houses are made of branches and grass held together with plaster made of cow urine and dung. This mixture is odorless after it dries in the sun. The Masai women build the houses. They also create beautiful bead-work, which is world famous.

Spiced Rice and Fresh Salad

For Kenya's Muslim population, Ramadan, a month-long religious celebration, marks a time to fast and a time to feast with family and friends. During Ramadan, Muslims fast from dawn to dusk each day. Each night a huge feast is served and everyone is welcome. **Pilau** (pi-la-u) is often on the table. This richly scented stew is made with rice cooked in coconut milk and flavored with cinnamon, cardamom, cloves, cumin, and garlic. Juicy beef chunks, golden fried onions, tomatoes, and black-eyed peas are added to the aromatic rice. While it is cooking, the air fills with an amazing aroma. It is a familiar scent to Kenyans, who have been combining these spices with coconut milk since the Arab traders introduced the spices to Kenya centuries ago. Indeed, the dish itself has its roots in the Middle East and in India. Kenyans are happy it found its way to Kenya.

Pilau tastes both sweet and zesty. Kenyans love the dish. It is served not only during Ramadan, but

These Kenyan women in Mombasa prepare a Ramadan feast.

also for special occasions. For many Kenyans, a platter of pilau symbolizes good times, celebrations, hospitality, and generosity. Kenyans, according to Kenyan writer Mary Otieno, "are known for their generosity. Cooking of pilau is one way of expressing this generosity. . . . One cooks pilau for the people he treasures most. Pilau is also cooked during special occasions like in weddings, birthday parties, anniversaries, or any other occasion that calls for celebrations."[19]

Pilau is almost always served with **kachumbari** (kach-oum-bah-ree), a chilled vegetable dish that is a cross between salad and relish. There are many different ways to make kachumbari. Typically it is made with farm-fresh tomatoes, hot peppers, onions, and cabbage. The vegetables are tossed with freshly squeezed lemon juice and sprinkled with coriander. Then the

Pilau is a richly scented stew made with rice cooked in coconut milk and flavored with cinnamon, cardamom, cloves, cumin, and garlic.

Kachumbari

Kachumbari is easy to make. The ingredients are flexible. To make it spicier add more hot peppers. Shredded carrots and sliced cucumber can also be added.

Ingredients
1 jalapeño pepper, seeds removed, chopped into
   small pieces
½ onion, chopped
4 Roma tomatoes, chopped
1 cup cabbage, shredded
juice of 1 lemon
salt to taste

Directions
1. Combine all the ingredients in a large bowl. Mix well.
2. Cover the bowl with foil or plastic wrap and refrigerate for a half hour.
3. Serve cold.
Serves 2.

dish is chilled for about twenty minutes before it is served. It makes a refreshing side dish for pilau or any other holiday favorite.

Sweet Endings

Even on special occasions, Kenyans usually do not eat pastries for dessert. They prefer fresh fruit. For festive meals, they prepare the fruit in special ways. Beautiful fruit trays laden with chunks of pineapple, mango, banana, and other tropical fruits are an artistic way to end celebratory dinners and a delightful treat to serve with tea whenever guests drop by.

Grilled pineapple slices marinated in coconut milk, sugar, and cinnamon is another delectable celebratory dessert. Bananas steamed and rolled in crunchy peanuts is a dish known as n'dizi (d-zee). Homemade sorbet or ice cream is also quite popular. Combinations like mango and passion fruit or mango and orange sorbet are simple to make. Cooks puree the fruits in a blender then freeze them to make a sweet, yet tangy, end to any meal.

Mangos are also featured in Kenya's version of an ice cream sundae, called Coupe Mount Kenya. It consists of rich, creamy, mango ice cream bathed in pineapple syrup and crowned with crushed pistachio nuts. It is sweet, salty, tangy, velvety, and crunchy all at the same

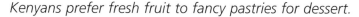

Kenyans prefer fresh fruit to fancy pastries for dessert.

Coupe Mount Kenya

Mango ice cream is usually used in this dish. Peach or vanilla ice cream is especially tasty too. Sorbet may be substituted for ice cream.

Ingredients
4   scoops ice cream
1   cup pineapple juice
3   cups pineapple chunks (fresh or canned), diced
1   cup sugar
2   tablespoons pistachio nuts, shelled and halved

Directions
1. Heat the pineapple juice and sugar in a saucepan over low heat. Stir often until a syrup forms.
2. Pour the syrup over the diced pineapple. Let it marinate for 1 hour.
3. Put the ice cream in four small bowls, one scoop per bowl. Top each scoop with the pineapples and a sprinkle of pistachio nuts.

Serves 4.

time. And the fragrance is irresistible. According to writer Paul Ndetei, when Coupe Mount Kenya is served at any dinner party, it "makes this a dinner people will talk about for a long time."[20]

Foods like Coupe Mount Kenya, kuku na nazi, karamu chicken, pilau, and kachumbari make any meal something to talk about. In Kenya these dishes make festive occasions all the more memorable and make guests feel that they are warmly welcomed.

Metric conversions

Mass (weight)

1 ounce (oz.)	= 28.0 grams (g)
8 ounces	= 227.0 grams
1 pound (lb.) or 16 ounces	= 0.45 kilograms (kg)
2.2 pounds	= 1.0 kilogram

Liquid Volume

1 teaspoon (tsp.)	= 5.0 milliliters (ml)
1 tablespoon (tbsp.)	= 15.0 milliliters
1 fluid ounce (oz.)	= 30.0 milliliters
1 cup (c.)	= 240 milliliters
1 pint (pt.)	= 480 milliliters
1 quart (qt.)	= 0.96 liters (l)
1 gallon (gal.)	= 3.84 liters

Pan Sizes

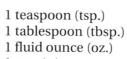

8- inch cake pan	= 20 x 4-centimeter cake pan
9-inch cake pan	= 23 x 3.5-centimeter cake pan
11 x 7-inch baking pan	= 28 x 18-centimeter baking pan
13 x 9-inch baking pan	= 32.5 x 23-centimeter baking pan
9 x 5-inch loaf pan	= 23 x 13-centimeter loaf pan
2-quart casserole	= 2-liter casserole

Temperature

212° F	= 100° C (boiling point of water)
225° F	= 110° C
250° F	= 120° C
275° F	= 135° C
300° F	= 150° C
325° F	= 160° C
350° F	= 180° C
375° F	= 190° C
400° F	= 200° C

Length

1/4 inch (in.)	= 0.6 centimeters (cm)
1/2 inch	= 1.25 centimeters
1 inch	= 2.5 centimeters

Notes

Chapter 1: A Land of Contrasts

1. Reay Tannahill, *Food in History*, New York: Crown, 1988, p. 205.

2. Iris Hunt, "Kenya Corn-Bacon Muffins," Mount Kenya Wildlife Conservatory, October 2003, www.animal orphanagekenya.org/members/african_recipe_corn_ bacon_muffins.php.

3. John Makeni, "Kenya: Traditional Foods on Top Hotel Menus," AllAfrica.com, January 13, 2008, http://allafrica .com/stories/200801140523.html.

4. Iris Hunt, "Cold Avocado Soup," Mount Kenya Wildlife Conservatory, August 2003, www.animalorphanagekenya.org/ members/african_recipe_avocado_soup.php.

5. Siggi, "Kenya Recipes," Kenya Travel Ideas, www.kenya travelideas.com/kenya-recipes.html.

Chapter 2: Many Influences

6. Kenya Tourist Board, "Our Culture," Magical Kenya, www .magicalkenya.com/index.php?option=com_content&task= view&id=26&Itemid=19.

7. Dorinda Hafner, *A Taste of Africa*, Berkeley, CA: Ten Speed Press, 2002, p. 102.

8. Pranay B. Gupte, "Currying Favor in Kenya," New York Times, February 29, 1982, www.nytimes.com/1982/02/28/ travel/currying-favor-in-kenya.html.

9. Lonely Planet, "Nyama Choma Place," restaurant review,

Lonely Planet, www.lonelyplanet.com/kenya/nairobi/restaurants/415648.

Chapter 3: All Kinds of Snacks

10. Joseph Bindloss, Tom Parkinson, and Matt Fletcher, *Kenya*, Victoria, Australia: Lonely Planet, 2003, p. 73.

11. Robin Kear, "Africa: Monday March 24, 2003," www.robinkear.com, March 24, 2003, www.robinkear.com/travels/africablog/archive/2003_03_01_archive.html.

12. Rachel Ngondo, "Fair Trade Tea and Kenya," SharedInterest, http://blog.shared-interest.com/?p=38#respond.

13. Swoosh, "How to Make Chai," African Wanderings, www.africanwanderings.com/?page_id=16.

14. Jeanne Egbosiuba Ukwendu, "Kenyan Chai Recipe," Bella-Online, www.bellaonline.com/articles/art2643.asp.

15. Jeanne Egbosiuba Ukwendu, "Mandazi Recipe: East African Donuts," BellaOnline, www.bellaonline.com/articles/art7250.asp.

16. Harva Hachten, *Best African Regional Cooking*, New York: Hippocrene, 1998, p. 224.

Chapter 4: Welcome! Welcome!

17. Tom Wfaula Kingoro, KIDSICO, "Kenyan Culture," KIDSICO, http://kidsico.bravehost.com/volunteer.html.

18. Quoted in "Kenyan Cuisine: Hospitality Management Student Pens African Cookbook," May 6, 2002, Polycentric, http://www.csupomona.edu/~polycentric/campus_news/050602-mbugua1.shtml.

19. Mary Otieno, "How to Cook Pilau," How To, http://calstaging.bemidjistate.edu/students/motieno/howto.html.

20. Paul Ndetei, "About Kenya," Teach Abroad, www.teacha-broad.biz/aboutkenya.html.

Glossary

chai: Sweet, milky, black tea.

chapati: A soft flatbread.

githeri: A popular stew.

irio: A popular dish made with corn and beans.

kachumbari: A Kenyan salad.

karamu: The Swahili word for feast.

Kikuyu: Kenya's largest ethnic group.

kuku na nazi: Chicken cooked in coconut milk.

maandazi: A fried sweet bread.

Masai: A Kenyan tribal group who herd cattle and live a traditional lifestyle.

maize: The Kenyan name for corn.

matokes: Small bananas that are very popular in Kenya.

nyama choma: Grilled meat.

pilau: Spiced rice.

plantains: Large green bananas that need to be cooked before they are eaten.

sambusa: A small pastry filled with meat or vegetables.

samp: Dried corn.

shamba: A small vegetable garden.

sukuma wiki: A popular stew made with kale or other greens.

Swahili: A cultural group formed when Arab traders married native Kenyans; also a language.

ugali: A cornmeal mush that Kenyans eat at almost every meal.

uji: A thin porridge made with cornmeal.

for further Exploration

Books

Sean McCollum, *Kenya*. Minneapolis, MN: Lerner, 2007. A fairly simple book with general information about Kenya. It includes maps and pictures.

Barbara Saffer, *Kenya: The Culture*. New York: Crabtree, 2006. General information about Kenya with a focus on the culture.

Web Sites

Africa for Kids (http://pbskids.org/africa). Africa for Kids is part of the larger PBS Kids Web site. The "My World" section of Africa for Kids features four schools in Africa, including Cannon Kituri School in Wundanyi, Kenya. Information about the school and its students is offered along with photos.

Fact Monster (www.factmonster.com/ipka/A0107678 .html). This is a reference site for students ages eight to fourteen. It includes an encyclopedia, a dictionary, an atlas, and several almanacs as well as information on a variety of subjects, such as people, sports, science, and geography. It also offers a profile for every country, including Kenya.

Food in Every Country (www.foodbycountry.com). This site provides recipes and information about food in different countries, including Kenya.

Kenya Information Guide (www.kenya-information-guide.com). This Web site offers all kinds of information about Kenya, including history, wildlife, tribes, culture, national parks, cities, and food with links to Kenyan recipes.

Magical Kenya (www.magicalkenya.com). This is the official Web site of the Kenya Tourist Board. It has lots of great information and pictures.

Mount Kenya Wildlife Conservatory (www .animalorphanagekenya.org). This is the Web site of the Mount Kenya Wildlife Conservatory, located in Nanyuki, Kenya. It is a home for orphaned and injured animals. The Web site offers lots of information about Kenyan wildlife, life in Kenya, and Kenyan food, including many different recipes.

Index

Picture Credits

Cover Photo: Nico Tondini/ Robert Harding Picture Library Ltd/ Alamy© Aflo Co. Ltd./Alamy, 26

© blickwinkel/Alamy, 6

© Bon Appetit/Alamy, 50

© Borderlands/Alamy, 47

© Mark Boulton/Alamy, 39, 42

© dbimages/Alamy, 14-15

Image copyright Anton Foltin, 2009. Used under license from Shutterstock.com, 8

© Gaba/G&B Images/Alamy, 38

Gale, Cengage Learning, 5

Image copyright Joe Gough, 2009. Used under license from Shutterstock.com, 48

Image copyright JackK, 2009. Used under license from Shutterstock.com, 12

Image copyright Kesu, 2009. Used under license from Shutterstock.com, 45

© Tina Manley/Africa/Alamy, 9

Image copyright Nanka (Kucherenko Olena), 2009. Used under license from Shutterstock.com, 25

© Daphne Ouwersloot/Alamy, 43

© Robert Harding Picture Library Ltd/Alamy, 19

Image copyright Elzbieta Sekowska, 2009. Used under license from Shutterstock.com, 21

© Frantisek Staud/Alamy, 33

Image copyright Carmen Steiner, 2009. Used under license from Shutterstock.com, 31

Image copyright Vinicius Tupinamba, 2009. Used under license from Shutterstock.com., 16

© Ariadne Van Zandbergen/Alamy, 28

About the Author

Barbara Sheen is the author of more than 50 books for young people. She lives in New Mexico with her family. In her spare time, she likes to swim, walk, garden, and read. Of course, she loves to cook!